AF228310

Searchlight BOOKS™

World Traveler

Travel to Colombia

Christine Layton

Lerner Publications ◆ Minneapolis

For Carrie and Polly

Consultant: Sarah C. Chambers, PhD, Professor of Latin American History
at the University of Minnesota

Lerner Publications Company
An imprint of Lerner Publishing Group, Inc.
241 First Avenue North
Minneapolis, MN 55401 USA

For reading levels and more information, look up this title
at www.lernerbooks.com.

Main body text set in Adrianna Regular.
Typeface provided by Chank.

Map illustration on page 29 by Laura K. Westlund.

Library of Congress Cataloging-in-Publication Data

Names: Layton, Christine Marie, 1985– author.
Title: Travel to Colombia / Christine Layton.
Description: Minneapolis : Lerner Publications, [2023] | Series: Searchlight books :
    world traveler | Includes bibliographical references and index. | Audience: Ages 8–11 |
    Audience: Grades 4–6 | Summary: "From the Andes Mountains to the Amazon,
    Colombia is full of culture and beauty. Follow the story of Colombia and learn how it
    became one of the most diverse and captivating countries in the world"— Provided
    by publisher.
Identifiers: LCCN 2022034606 (print) | LCCN 2022034607 (ebook) |
    ISBN 9781728491608 (lib. bdg.) | ISBN 9798765600597 (eb pdf)
Subjects: LCSH: Colombia—Juvenile literature.
Classification: LCC F2258.5 .L39 2023 (print) | LCC F2258.5 (ebook) | DDC 986.1—
    dc23/eng/20220722

LC record available at https://lccn.loc.gov/2022034606
LC ebook record available at https://lccn.loc.gov/2022034607

Manufactured in the United States of America
1-53099-51109-10/24/2022

Table of Contents

GEOGRAPHY AND CLIMATE

Colombia is one of the largest countries in South America. The country is home to many different landscapes and diverse cultures. Condors fly high in the Andes Mountains. Giant anteaters and jaguars walk the eastern grasslands. Coffee farms stretch across the northwest.

Land

Colombia connects South America to Central America. Colombia borders Panama to the northwest and touches Ecuador to the southwest, Peru to the south, Brazil to the southeast, and Venezuela to the east. It borders the Caribbean Sea to the north and the Pacific Ocean to the west.

The Andes Mountains rise through central Colombia. The north and west coasts have tropical beaches. The north also has deserts. Large grasslands called Los Llanos lie in the east. The tropical rain forest of the Amazon basin forms the southern border. The northwest also has a jungle forest, the Chocó.

Rivers and Lakes

Colombia's longest rivers are the Río Negro, the largest tributary of the Amazon River, and the Orinoco in the west. Tributaries of the Amazon River also flow through the country and empty into the Atlantic Ocean. The Magdalena is an important river system that covers a quarter of the country. The Magdalena flows north from the Andes to the Caribbean.

Hydroelectric plants, such as the Hidroituango, use river water to power about 70 percent of the country. But severe weather such as droughts and floods can cause problems.

Must-See Stop:
Tayrona National Park

The highest coastal mountain in the world meets the Caribbean Sea in Tayrona National Park. Clear water laps on bays, coves, and white sand beaches. Mangrove swamps, bushes, and forests surround the area. Tourists visit the park to snorkel and dive. The area also has archaeological ruins. Visitors can see an ancient city of the Indigenous Tayrona people.

Climate

Colombia has a tropical climate. On the coasts and in the south, Colombia's average temperature is about 75°F (23.9°C) and the average rainfall is 8.6 feet (2.6 m). The Chocó region has more than three hundred days of rain a year with 33 feet (10 m) of rain annually. The highest peaks have an average temperature below 50°F (10°C). The dry season lasts from November to April. The wet rainy season lasts from May to October.

COFFEE FARM RANCH OF
THE COCORA VALLEY

Chapter 2

HISTORY AND GOVERNMENT

Archaeologists have discovered paintings on cliff walls in the Amazon rain forest that show life twelve thousand years ago in Colombia. The paintings show people doing activities such as dancing and jumping from wooden towers.

One of the largest groups was the Chibcha, which included many ethnic groups and states. Larger Chibcha villages had markets to sell farm produce, pottery, and cotton cloth. The Chibcha also traded for gold to make ornaments and religious offerings.

By the 1500s, Colombia was home to about two million people belonging to hundreds of tribes.

Must-See Stop:
San Agustín Archaeological Park

San Agustín Archaeological Park is a historical park in the southwest Andes. The park holds the largest group of megalithic statues in South America. These statues of gods and animals were carved from volcanic stone sometime between the first and eighth century CE. Visitors can view the ancient statues and burial mounds as well as tour the park's archaeological museum.

Spanish Colonization

In 1492, Christopher Columbus's voyage from Spain to the West Indies began a wave of European exploration in South America. From 1510 to 1550, Spanish conquistadors claimed land for Spain even though many Indigenous peoples were living there. The Spanish called this empire the Viceroyalty of New Granada. The Spanish enslaved African people and brought them to this new colony. Enslaved Africans and Indigenous peoples were forced to work in gold mines, on sugarcane plantations, and in Spanish homes.

Spanish explorers also brought Catholicism to Colombia. The church provided schools and health care. The new religion was forced on many Indigenous peoples and in most cases replaced their native religions.

Independence

For nearly 250 years, conquistadors ruled the government, took Colombia's resources, and enslaved its people. In 1808, France invaded Spain and captured the Spanish king Ferdinand VII. While the king was gone, the people of New Granada declared their independence from Spain. Revolutionary leaders Simón Bolívar, José Antonio Páez, and Francisco de Paula Santander marched into Bogotá and defeated the Spanish on August 10, 1819.

In 1819, Colombia, Panama, Venezuela, and Ecuador united to become one country, Gran Colombia. Bolívar became its president. But Páez, Santander, and Bolívar could not agree on a constitution for Gran Colombia.

The Battle of Boyacá ended in victory for the forces of New Granada and allowed Simón Bolívar to capture Bogotá three days later.

Fighting led to civil war. In 1803, Venezuela and Ecuador seceded from Colombia. Panama remained part of Colombia until 1903, when it declared independence with the support of the US, which was interested in building a canal through the country.

Political leaders continued to fight over who should lead the country. Colombia had several more civil wars from 1900 to the 2000s. In 2016, Colombian president Juan Manuel Santos earned the Nobel Peace Prize for his efforts to end a fifty-year civil war.

Juan Manuel Santos served for eight years as Colombia's president.

Let's Celebrate!
Carnaval de Negros y Blancos

The Carnaval de Negros y Blancos lasts from December 28 to January 6. The festival includes a mix of African, Indigenous Andean, and Hispanic traditions. People burn paper dolls that represent people and events from the past to say goodbye to the old year.

People paint their faces during the last two days. The event celebrates how people of different backgrounds and cultures have come together to make the Colombian culture.

Capitolio Nacional, Colombia's national capitol building, was finished in 1926. It stands in Bolívar Square in Bogotá.

Government

Colombia is a presidential republic with three branches. The president, elected by the people every four years, runs the executive branch. The legislative branch creates laws. It has a House of Representatives and a Senate. The judicial branch interprets and applies the laws.

Chapter 3

CULTURE AND PEOPLE

Colombia is home to about fifty million people. According to a 2015 census, about 10 percent of Colombia's population is Afro-Colombian, the descendants of enslaved Africans. About 4 percent of the population is Amerindian, the descendants of Indigenous peoples. Nearly 86 percent of the population is mestizo. They have a mix of European and Amerindian ancestors.

Food

The food in Colombia is as diverse as its people. Arepas are grilled, fried, roasted, or boiled. These corn cakes are often stuffed with meat or cheese. Bandeja paisa is a traditional Colombian dish made of rice, beans, egg, avocado, arepa, plantains, and meat.

There are many local varieties of arepas in Colombia, such as the sweet arepa boyacense or the arepa de huevo of the Caribbean coast.

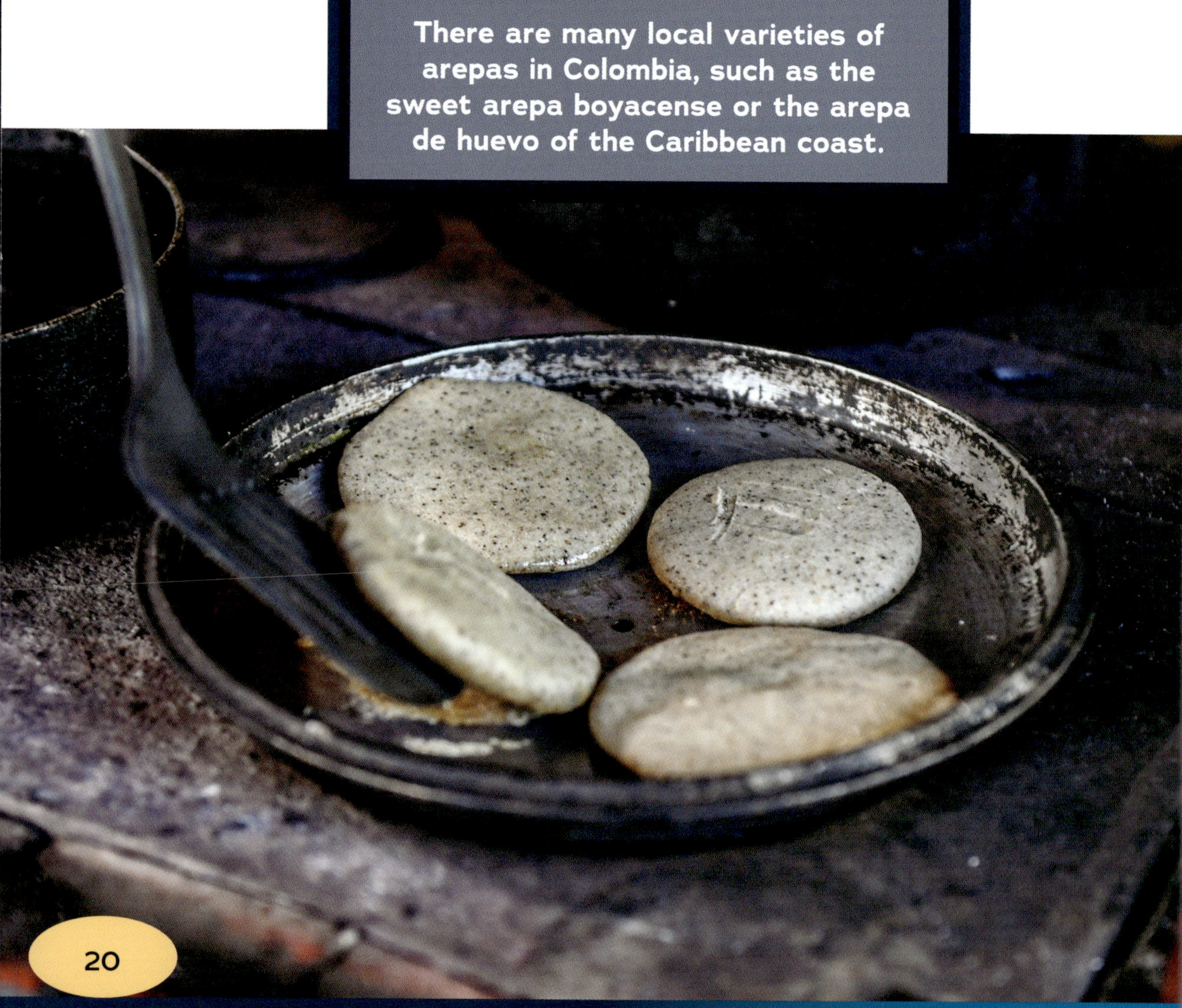

Other foods show the culture of a region. Ranchers in the Los Llanos region raise cattle, so they eat barbecued beef. The northern coasts serve fresh seafood with spicy Caribbean flavors along with coconut rice. Mote de queso con hogao is a yam and cheese soup with a mix of African and Spanish flavors.

Let's Celebrate!

Carnaval de Barranquilla

Lent is the forty days before Easter when some Christians sacrifice by fasting or giving up meat on certain days. Each year for four days before Lent begins, Colombians celebrate Carnival. The biggest Carnival celebration is Carnaval de Barranquilla.

Colombians celebrate Carnival with dances and music from many cultures. People celebrate by making handmade crafts such as animal masks and decorations for parade floats. Dancers, actors, singers, and musicians perform events from Colombia's history.

Music and Dance

Colombia has a wide variety of music. Cumbia is a traditional music and dance that combines African drums with Amerindian flutes. In the Andes region, people enjoy traditional music called bambuco. It sounds like Spanish guitar music mixed with drumbeats from currulao. Currulao is a music and dance style from the Pacific region. Enslaved Africans who were forced to Colombia invented it. Traditional song lyrics are often about the natural world, while newer songs deal with politics and current events.

Chapter 4

DAILY LIFE

Most Colombians live in the north and west. Some ranchers live in the eastern grasslands. Some Amerindian peoples live in the Amazon basin, including the Cabillarí, Tanimukas, Letuamas Yahunas, and many others.

Bogotá is the largest city. It has a population of 11.34 million people. Medellín and Barranquilla are other large cities. Many people in cities work at food processing plants, clothing manufacturing sites, hotels, restaurants, and shops.

Built in the sixteeth century, the Church of St. Francis in Bogotá is one of the oldest churches in Colombia.

Rural Colombians are more likely to face economic barriers. Jobs are harder to find, so people are more likely to have more than one job and travel to find work. Schools and hospitals can be far from remote villages.

Colombia is the fourth-largest producer of oil in Latin America and the eleventh-largest producer of coal in the world. Colombia also exports gold, silver, platinum, and emeralds. Agricultural exports include sugarcane, bananas, and cassava leaves. Colombia is the world's third-largest coffee exporter and second-largest flower exporter.

Must-See Stop:
Sanctuary of Monserrate

The Sanctuary of Monserrate is in the hills of Bogotá. People see the building from most places in the city. Visitors walk 2 miles (3.2 km) uphill to reach it.

In 1620, people began visiting the sanctuary to see the shrine of Our Lady of Monserrate. The shrine has a statue of Christ. Religious followers say the statue performs miracles. Every weekend, Colombians and tourists climb the path to the Sanctuary of Monserrate.

Climate change threatens Colombia's natural resources and people. Drought affects people in the Andes where water is scarce. Rising sea levels affect people who live on the coast. Changes in temperature and rainfall can hurt agriculture across Colombia.

To help fight climate change and poverty in Colombia, the government wrote a National Development Plan in 2018. The plan is meant to lessen the number of

The Suesca lagoon, a popular tourist attraction, has begun to disappear due to droughts caused by climate change.

Colombians living on low incomes, improve education, and protect the environment. Colombians will plant 180 million trees to try to fight pollution and threats to the Amazon rain forest.

Colombia's people are coming together to help its economy and environment, creating a bright future for one of the most beautiful and diverse countries in the world.

Map and Key Facts

Flag of
Colombia

- **Continent: South America**
- **Capital city: Bogotá**
- **Population: 49,059,221**
- **Languages: Spanish, English, and many Indigenous languages**

Glossary

ancestor: a person from whom someone is descended

archaeologist: someone who studies human history and prehistory by digging up old objects

civil war: a war between different groups in the same country

conquistador: a leader in the Spanish conquest of Central and South America in the sixteenth century

export: to send products to another country to sell them

indigenous: living, existing, or produced originally or naturally in a particular region or environment

megalith: a large stone used in prehistoric cultures as a monument or building block

mestizo: a person of mixed European and Amerindian ancestry

Learn More

Britannica Kids: Colombia
https://kids.britannica.com/kids/article/Colombia/345667

Golkar, Golriz. *Colombia*. Minneapolis: Bellwether Media, 2021.

Kids World Travel Guide: Colombia
https://www.kids-world-travel-guide.com/colombia-facts.html

Layton, Christine. *Travel to Brazil*. Minneapolis: Lerner Publications, 2023.

National Geographic Kids: Colombia
https://kids.nationalgeographic.com/geography/countries/article/colombia

Regan, Michael. *South America*. Lake Elmo: Focus Readers, 2021.

Index

Photo Acknowledgments

Image credits: Tor Eigeland/Alamy Stock Photo, p. 5; Juan David Moreno Gallego/Anadolu Agency/Getty Images, p. 6; Alex Saberi/Getty Images, p. 7; Edinson Ivan Arroyo Mora/Bloomberg/Getty Images, p. 8; Fred Fraces/Getty Images, p. 9; Photos.com/Getty Images, p. 11; Victor Ovies Arenas/Getty Images, p. 12; Art Heritage/Alamy Stock Photo, p. 13; Blake Callahan/Getty Images, p. 14; Heritage Image Partnership Ltd/Alamy Stock Photo, p. 15; Ovidio Gonzalez/Getty Images, p. 16; Elizabeth Palchucan/Long Visual Press/Universal Images Group/Getty Images, p. 17; travel4pictures/Alamy Stock Photo, p. 18; LUIS ACOSTA/AFP/Getty Images, p. 20; JOAQUIN SARMIENTO/AFP/Getty Images, p. 21; David Moran/Anadolu Agency/Getty Images, p. 22; Gustavo Adolfo Delvasto Daza/Anadolu Agency/Getty Images, p. 23; John Coletti/Getty Images, p. 25; imageBROKER/Alamy Stock Photo, p. 26; RAUL ARBOLEDA/AFP/Getty Images, p. 27; LUIS ACOSTA/AFP/Getty Images, p. 28; Laura Westlund, p. 29.

Cover: Claudio Sieber/Getty Images.